Anti-Inflammatory and Detox Cookbook for Beginners

How to Strengthen Your Immune System and Rejuvenate
Your Body With 365 Days of Delicious and Easy Recipes

Britney Kim

Table of Contents

INTRODUCTION

An anti-inflammatory diet has recently become quite a rage as it provides many health benefits and weight loss. It is a journey that will help you transform yourself into a healthy being through nutrient-rich and delicious foods. This book contains a curated collection of mouth-watering recipes that can excite your taste buds and help your body tackle inflammation. Through this diet, you will be able to experience a new form of vitality, health, and energy through the medium of the right and nutrient-rich foods.

Inflammation is a naturally occurring immune response triggered by the body in certain cases. It is both good and bad according to the situation. For instance, acute inflammation is an important defense mechanism of the body that can protect the body from foreign objects and harmful conditions such as injuries and infections.

While acute inflammation is generally positive, chronic inflammation can be quite a problem. Inflammation occurs due to a variety of reasons. It can also be a gateway to diseases and disorders such as cardiovascular disease, diabetes, arthritis, and even cancer. Other conditions, like rheumatoid arthritis, psoriasis, asthma, etc., often accompany chronic inflammation.

Inflammation can often become worse due to certain foods. This fact makes inflammation quite scary. But the good news is that changing your diet and lifestyle can influence your body and change the inflammatory response according to your requirements. Avoiding or limiting certain foods such as red meat, processed foods, and alcohol and increasing the intake of other natural, plant-based foods can help you tackle inflammation.

Diseases such as psoriasis, rheumatoid arthritis, and asthma cause chronic inflammation. An anti-inflammatory diet focuses on vegetables, fruits, and foods with omega-3 fatty acids, lean protein, whole grains, spices, and healthful fats and recommends avoiding or at least reducing the intake of red meats, processed foods, and alcohol.

As it is clear from the description, an anti-inflammatory diet is not a specific diet or a regimen in the modern sense of the term 'diet.' Rather it is a style or method of eating. Many 'diets' can be considered anti-inflammatory, including the DASH and Mediterranean diets.

Why Do Some Foods Trigger Inflammation?

While it is clear that processed foods, red meats, sugary foods, and alcohol can trigger inflammation, the science behind this trigger is quite interesting too.

Specific foods contain chemicals that are either good or bad for your health. For instance, fresh veggies and fruits contain a lot of dietary antioxidant molecules, which are considered good for the body. On the other hand, foods such as processed foods can trigger the formation of free radicals in the body, which are considered to be quite harmful to the body.

By focusing on fresh veggies and fruits and reducing the intake of processed foods, an anti-inflammatory diet allows your body to get more antioxidants and fewer free radicals. But not all antioxidants can reduce the number of free radicals already present in the body. Along with processed foods, other things, such as smoking, stress, etc., can also increase the number of free radicals in your body.

Free radicals are harmful as they lead to cell damage and inflammation, which can ultimately be a gateway for many diseases.

While the body naturally produces antioxidants to tackle these toxins, consuming dietary antioxidants can expedite the process of removal.

Other healthy molecules, such as omega-3 fatty acids, can help you reduce inflammation. Oily fish such as salmon contains high amounts of omega-3 fatty acids.

Who Should Follow An Anti-inflammatory Diet?

Ideally, anyone and everyone can follow an anti-inflammatory diet as it is supposed to be healthy for everyone. It can be used as a complementary therapy for many conditions and a good method for losing weight. Here are some conditions that can be resolved (to a large extent) with the help of an anti-inflammatory diet:

- Asthma
- Rheumatoid Arthritis
- Psoriasis
- Colitis
- Crohn's Disease, Lupus
- Eosinophilic esophagitis
- Inflammatory bowel disease
- Hashimoto's thyroiditis

Metabolic syndrome includes a combination of conditions that are present together. Some of these conditions are obesity, type 2 diabetes, cardiovascular diseases, high blood pressure and more.

An anti-inflammatory diet can also reduce the risk of certain types of cancers.

Anti-Inflammatory Diet: What to Eat and What Not to Eat

Foods to Eat

Here is a list of foods you should eat while following an anti-inflammatory diet. Remember that no single food can work like magic, and you need to consume various foods for the best results. A plate should be as colorful as possible (natural colors and no additives). This will provide you with ample antioxidants and other nutrients too. Consume as many varieties of vegetables and fruits as possible and try to consume fresh and simple ingredients. Avoid processed foods as much as possible, even if they contain natural ingredients. For instance, while cocoa is considered to be a good food if bought premade, it may often contain excess fat and sugar, which in turn needs to be avoided.

To sum up, you should ideally eat foods that contain various levels of antioxidants, are rich in nutrients, and contain large amounts of healthful fats.

List:

- Fruits include strawberries, blackberries, cherries, blueberries, etc.
- Vegetables including green and leafy veggies such as spinach, kale, and broccoli
- Oily fish such as salmon and tuna.
- Nuts, beans, and seeds
- Healthy oils such as olive oil and olives.
- A diet rich in fiber
- Legumes including lentils
- Raw veggies (or medium-cooked veggies)
- Probiotics and Prebiotics
- Black, green, and floral teas
- Spices including turmeric, ginger, etc.
- Fresh herbs

Foods to Avoid

Here is a list of foods you should avoid while following an anti-inflammatory diet. If you cannot avoid these completely, limiting their intake as much as possible is recommended.

List:

- Foods that contain added salt and sugar
- Processed foods
- Unhealthy oils
- Processed foods, including crackers and chips
- Processed carbs, including baked goods, white pasta, white bread, etc.
- Premade desserts, including candy, cookies, ice cream, etc.
- Excessive amounts of alcohol.

Along with these, you may also reduce the consumption of foods that contain the following elements:

Gluten

Some people may have an anti-inflammatory reaction after consuming gluten, even without having gluten energy. Such people should reduce the consumption of gluten. While it is difficult to follow a gluten-free diet, you can reduce the intake slowly and then discard it completely or at least until the symptoms improve.

Nightshades

Nightshade is a plant family that contains many deadly poisons and some common and popular edible fruits and vegetables, such as eggplants, tomatoes, potatoes, and peppers. It is recommended to reduce the nightshade intake to observe the changes in your body.

Carbohydrates

A high-carb diet, including carbs that are considered to be healthy, can increase inflammation in some people. But it is best to check it yourself as many foods are rich in carbs and contain high amounts of nutrients and antioxidants.

The anti-inflammatory diet is not a fad or a passing diet. It has gained significant recognition from researchers and users. It also makes sense to consume natural and plant-based foods and reduce the intake of unhealthy foods such as processed foods.

So, if you want to try your hand at the anti-inflammatory diet, don't wait; get your apron on, sharpen your tools, and jump right into the world of mouthwatering and healthy recipes that can help you deliciously tackle inflammation. Your path to a healthier, happier life begins right here.

CHAPTER 1:
BREAKFAST RECIPES

Pineapple Grapefruit Detox Smoothie

Serves: 1

Nutritional values per serving: 1 smoothie

Calories: 102

Fat: 0.2 g

Carbohydrates: 25.2 g

Protein: 2 g

Ingredients:

- ½ cup coconut water
- ½ cup packed baby spinach
- ½ inch ginger, peeled, grated
- ½ cup frozen diced pineapple
- ½ small grapefruit, peeled, separated into segments, deseeded

- Ice cubes, as required

Directions:

1. Make this smoothie just before drinking it. Blend spinach, ginger, pineapple, coconut water, grapefruit, and ice cubes in a blender for about a minute or until the preferred consistency. Serve immediately.

Spicy Anti-Inflammatory Smoothie

Serves: 2

Nutritional values per serving: 1 smoothie

Calories: 266

Fat: 13 g

Carbohydrates: 41 g

Protein: 4 g

Ingredients:

- 2 cups freshly brewed green tea, cooled to room temperature
- 1 cup fresh or frozen papaya chunks
- 1 cup fresh or frozen cherries, pitted
- 2 cups baby spinach
- 1 cup fresh or frozen blueberries

- ⅔ avocado, peeled, pitted, chopped
- ½ tablespoon chia seeds
- 1 teaspoon ground ginger
- 1 teaspoon ground cinnamon
- 2 teaspoons honey
- 2 teaspoons turmeric powder or 2-inch pieces fresh turmeric, peeled, sliced
- ½ teaspoon cayenne pepper
- A pinch of salt
- 1 tablespoon coconut oil

Directions:

2. Add green tea, papaya, cherries, spinach, blueberries, avocado, chia seeds, spices, honey, and salt into a blender.
3. Blend for 30-40 seconds or until smooth.
4. Pour into two glasses and serve with ice.

Pink Power Smoothie

Serves: 2

Nutritional values per serving: 1 smoothie without protein powder

Calories: 278

Fat: 5.6 g

Carbohydrates: 37.2 g

Protein: 6.2 g

Ingredients:

- 2 cups unsweetened almond milk
- 2 small beets, peeled, chopped
- 2 tablespoons flaxseed meal
- 2 scoops vanilla protein powder (optional)
- 2 bananas, sliced
- 2 cups frozen strawberries

- 2 teaspoons raw honey

Directions:

5. Blend banana, strawberries, beets, milk, honey, and flaxseed meal in a blender until smooth. Add protein powder if using and blend until well combined.
6. Pour into two glasses and serve.

Breakfast Salad

Serves: 2

Nutritional values per serving: ½ recipe

Calories: 527

Fat: 34 g

Carbohydrates: 37 g

Protein: 16 g

Ingredients:

- 6 tablespoons salsa Verde
- ¼ cup chopped cilantro plus extra to garnish
- 16 blue corn tortilla chips break into big pieces
- ½ avocado, peeled, pitted, sliced
- 8 teaspoons extra-virgin olive oil, divided
- 4 cups salad greens of your choice

- 1 cup canned or cooked red kidney beans, rinsed, drained
- 2 large eggs

Directions:

7. Add salsa, cilantro, and 6 teaspoons of oil into a bowl and mix well.
8. Place salad greens in a bowl. Drizzle half the salsa mixture over the greens and toss well.
9. Add the remaining oil into a pan and place it over medium heat. Crack the eggs into the pan at different spots. Remove eggs from the pan when the whites are set and the yolks are cooked to your preference.
10. To assemble: Divide the salad greens into two bowls. Layer the greens with half of each- chips followed by beans and finally avocado in each bowl.
11. Place an egg on top of each salad. Divide the remaining salsa mixture and spoon equally over the salad.
12. Garnish with some cilantro and serve.

Spinach and Egg Tacos

Serves: 2

Nutritional values per serving: 2 tacos

Calories: 421

Fat: 24 g

Carbohydrates: 32 g

Protein: 21 g

Ingredients:

- ½ avocado, mashed
- 4 hard-boiled eggs, peeled, chopped
- 2 cups chopped spinach
- 4 tablespoons salsa
- 2 teaspoon lime juice
- Salt to taste

- 4 corn tortillas warmed
- 4 tablespoons shredded cheddar cheese, divided

Directions:

1. Mix well with salt, lime juice, and avocado in a bowl.
2. Add eggs and stir. Distribute the egg mixture equally and place it over the tortillas.
3. Divide the spinach among the tortillas. Scatter 1 tablespoon of cheese on top, place a tablespoon of salsa over the spinach on each tortilla, and serve.

Savory Oatmeal with Cheddar and Fried Egg

Serves: 2

Nutritional values per serving: 1 bowl, without optional toppings

Calories: 262

Fat: 16 g

Carbohydrates: 18 g

Protein: 13 g

Ingredients:

- ½ cup of uncooked quick-cooking steel-cut oats
- ¼ teaspoon of salt
- 2 teaspoons of coconut oil divided
- ¼ teaspoon of pepper
- ¼ cup of finely chopped onion
- 1 ½ cups of water

- ¼ cup of shredded white cheddar cheese
- ½ cup of diced red bell pepper
- 2 large eggs

For the toppings (Optional):

- Thinly sliced green onions
- Chopped walnuts
- Za'atar spice blend

Directions:

1. Pour water into a small saucepan. Place the saucepan over high heat.
2. When the water starts boiling, stir in the oatmeal. Turn the heat to medium and constantly stir until the oats are cooked and there is no water in the saucepan.
3. Remove the saucepan from the heat. Add cheese, ⅛ teaspoon each of salt and pepper.
4. Meanwhile, add 1 teaspoon of coconut oil to a nonstick pan and let it heat over medium-high heat. When the oil melts, add onion and bell pepper and mix well.
5. Cook until the vegetables are tender. Add half of the remaining salt and mix well.
6. Divide the cooked oats into two bowls. Divide the vegetables equally and place them over the oats.
7. Cook the eggs sunny side up, using the remaining oil. Put the remaining salt and pepper over the eggs.
8. Place an egg in each bowl and serve with suggested toppings if using.

Breakfast Beans with Poached Egg

Serves: 1

Nutritional values per serving: 1 bowl

Calories: 364

Fat: 20 g

Carbohydrates: 32 g

Protein: 16 g

Ingredients:

- 1 teaspoon olive or canola oil
- 1 scallion, chopped (keep the whites and green separate)
- 6 tablespoons canned or cooked black beans, rinsed
- ¼ cup vegetable broth or chicken broth
- A dash of hot sauce
- 1 tablespoon shredded pepper Jack cheese

- 1 tablespoon chopped fresh cilantro
- ⅛ cup chopped red bell pepper
- ¼ teaspoon ground cumin
- ¼ cup cooked barley
- Salt to taste
- ¼ avocado peeled, pitted sliced
- 1 large egg
- ½ teaspoon vinegar
- ½ cup water

Directions:

1. Place a pan over medium heat. Add oil and let it heat. Add whites of the scallions, bell pepper, and cumin and stir. Cook for a couple of minutes.
2. Stir in broth, barley, beans, and salt, and cook until nearly dry.
3. Add scallion greens and hot sauce and stir. Turn off the heat and transfer it into a bowl. Keep the bowl covered until the egg is poached.
4. Add water and vinegar into a microwave-safe bowl. Crack the egg directly into the microwave bowl with water and vinegar. The egg should be immersed in the water. Cover the bowl and cook on high in the microwave for about 50 to 70 seconds or until the white is cooked and the yolk is runny.
5. Take out the poached egg with a slotted spoon and place it on top of the bean mixture, and serve.

Baked Oatmeal with Banana, Raisins, and Walnuts

Serves: 3

Nutritional values per serving: ⅓ recipe

Calories: 327

Fat: 13 g

Carbohydrates: 46 g

Protein: 9 g

Ingredients:

- 1 cup rolled oats
- ¾ teaspoon ground cinnamon
- ¼ teaspoon salt
- 1 cup of low-fat milk

- 1 tablespoon canola oil
- ½ teaspoon vanilla extract
- 3 tablespoons raisins
- 3 tablespoons chopped walnuts
- ½ teaspoon baking powder
- ⅛ teaspoon ground allspice
- 6 tablespoons low-fat plain yogurt
- 2 tablespoons packed light brown sugar
- ½ large banana, cut into semi-circle slices

Directions:

1. Preheat the oven to 375°F. Grease a small baking dish (about 5–6 inches) with cooking spray.
2. Add walnuts, oats, cinnamon, allspice, salt, and baking powder to a bowl and mix well.
3. Add milk, oil, vanilla, yogurt, and brown sugar into another bowl and stir until sugar dissolves. Turn off the heat.
4. Combine the milk mixture and oats mixture.
5. Add raisins and banana and stir. Spoon the mixture into the baking dish and place it in the oven for about 40 minutes or until the top is golden brown.
6. Cut into 3 equal portions and serve.

Granola Breakfast Protein Balls

Serves: 6

Nutritional values per serving: 1 ball

Calories: 148

Fat: 8 g

Carbohydrates: 4 g

Protein: 4 g

Ingredients:

- ¼ cup salted, creamy peanut butter
- ½ teaspoon vanilla extract
- ¼ cup granola
- ⅛ cup unsweetened toasted coconut flakes
- ⅛ cup coconut nectar or honey
- ½ cup old-fashioned oats

- ⅛ cup ground flax seeds

Directions:

1. Add peanut butter, vanilla, and coconut nectar into a bowl and whisk until smooth.
2. Combine the peanut butter mixture, oats, coconut flakes, granola, and flax seeds. Make 6 equal portions and form each into a ball.
3. Store the granola balls in an airtight container and place them in the refrigerator until use. They can last for a week. If you freeze the balls, they can last for a month.

Spinach-Mushroom Frittata with Avocado Salad

Serves: 2

Nutritional values per serving: ½ recipe

Calories: 415

Fat: 25 g

Carbohydrates: 30 g

Protein: 19 g

Ingredients:

For the salad:

- 1 tablespoon lemon juice
- 2 small cloves garlic, minced
- ⅛ teaspoon chili powder

- ⅛ teaspoon pepper
- ⅛ teaspoon ground cumin
- ⅛ teaspoon salt or to taste
- 2 teaspoons olive oil
- ½ medium cucumber chopped into ½ inch pieces
- ½ ripe avocado, peeled, pitted, cut into cubes
- 1 medium tomato, chopped into ½ inch pieces
- 1 tablespoon reduced-fat feta cheese, crumbled

For the frittata:

- 2 teaspoons olive oil, divided
- Salt to taste
- 2 scallions, thinly sliced
- ⅛ teaspoon pepper
- ¼ cup nonfat cottage cheese
- 1 medium Yukon gold potato, diced
- 1 cup sliced mushrooms
- 2 cups chopped baby spinach
- ⅛ teaspoon dried thyme
- 3 large eggs

Directions:

1. For the salad dressing: Add lemon juice, garlic, chili powder, pepper, oil, cumin, and salt into a bowl and whisk well.
2. To make salad: Combine cucumber, avocado, and tomatoes in a bowl.
3. Pour the dressing over the salad. Stir until well combined. Keep the bowl covered for the flavors to set in.
4. Meanwhile, make the frittata: Put the potatoes in a microwave-safe bowl. Cook covered in the microwave, on high, for about 3 to 4 minutes or until tender and can be pierced with a fork. Stir every minute or so.
5. Place a non-stick pan over medium heat. Add half of the oil and allow it to heat.

6. Add mushrooms to the hot oil. Season with salt and stir-fry until the moisture is released.
7. Add scallion, spinach, pepper, and thyme and mix well. Cook for a couple of minutes until the spinach turns limp.
8. Remove the spinach mixture into a bowl. Let it cool down.
9. Clean the pan and wipe it dry. Place it over medium heat. Add 1 teaspoon of oil and let it heat.
10. Add eggs and cottage cheese into a bowl and whisk until smooth.
11. Stir in the mushrooms and potatoes. Pour this mixture into the pan. Let it cook for a couple of minutes. Lift the edges with a spatula so that the uncooked eggs can flow beneath.
12. When the frittata is completely set, turn off the heat. Slice into wedges and place on individual serving plates. Place half the salad on each plate. Sprinkle feta on top and serve.

Pineapple Scones

Serves: 4

Nutritional values per serving: 1 scone

Calories: 235

Fat: 8 g

Carbohydrates: 39 g

Protein: 6 g

Ingredients:

- 1 ½ cups whole-wheat flour
- ½ teaspoon baking soda
- ½ tablespoon baking powder
- ¼ teaspoon salt
- 6 tablespoons of non-dairy milk of your choice
- 3 tablespoons coconut oil, frozen, cut into small pieces

- ½ can crushed pineapple, drained
- ½ tablespoon coconut sugar or brown sugar
- ½ tablespoon minced fresh rosemary
- ½ teaspoon lemon juice
- 1 ½ tablespoons maple syrup
- ½ teaspoon vanilla extract
- 1 tablespoon sliced almonds

Directions:

1. Firstly preheat the oven to 425 °F.
2. Combine the dry ingredients in a bowl, i.e. flour, salt, baking soda, and baking powder, and stir until well combined.
3. To make buttermilk: Add lemon juice and milk into another bowl and set aside for a few minutes. It will curdle, say, within 10 minutes. Stir in maple syrup.
4. Remove the frozen coconut oil cubes from the freezer just before using it. Add coconut oil cubes into the bowl of the flour mixture. Cut it into the mixture with a pastry cutter or with your hands until crumbly in texture.
5. Add the buttermilk a little at a time, and mix well each time.
6. Stir in the pineapple and vanilla. Mix until dough is formed.
7. Dust your countertop with some flour. Place the dough on your countertop and shape it into a ball.
8. Flatten the dough until it is a rectangle of 2 inches thick. Fold the dough into a quarter by first folding it in half and folding it once more in half.
9. Roll the dough using a rolling pin until it is 1 ½ inch thick rectangle.
10. Cut the rolled dough into 4 equal triangles. Place the scones on a baking sheet with parchment paper, leaving a sufficient gap between them.
11. Spray some cooking spray over the scones. Scatter coconut sugar, almonds, and rosemary.

12. Bake on the central rack in the oven for 10-15- minutes or until puffed up and golden brown.
13. Cool the scones on a wire rack for a few minutes and serve.

Breakfast Lemon, Raspberry, and Cream Cheese Cakes

Serves: 6

Nutritional values per serving: 1 cake

Calories: 140

Fat: 3 g

Carbohydrates: 24 g

Protein: 5 g

Ingredients:

- ⅛ cup reduced-fat cream cheese
- ½ teaspoon finely grated lemon zest
- 1 ½ cups old-fashioned rolled oats
- ½ cup fresh or frozen raspberries, divided
- ⅛ cup unsweetened applesauce

- ½ teaspoon baking powder
- ¼ teaspoon salt
- ½ tablespoon raspberry jam
- ½ teaspoon fresh lemon juice
- 10 tablespoons of low-fat milk
- 3 tablespoons packed brown sugar
- 1 large egg, lightly beaten
- ½ teaspoon vanilla extract

Directions:

1. Preheat the oven to 375 °F.
2. Grease a muffin pan of 6 counts with some cooking oil spray. Place disposable liners in the cups if desired.
3. Add cream cheese, lemon juice, and jam into a bowl and whisk until smooth.
4. Add oats, ¼ cup of raspberries, applesauce, baking powder, lemon zest, milk, brown sugar, egg, vanilla, and salt into a mixing bowl. Stir until well combined. As you stir, break up the raspberries into smaller pieces. Make sure the raspberries are well distributed in the mixture.
5. Place 2 tablespoons of the oats batter into each of the muffin cups. Divide the cream cheese mixture equally and place in each cup over the batter. Scatter a few of the remaining raspberries in each cup.
6. Now divide the remaining batter equally and place in the muffin cups over the cream cheese mixture.
7. Bake for 25 to 30 minutes or until cooked through. Insert a toothpick in the center of a cake (do not go up to the cream cheese layer) and take it out. If you find any batter stuck on the toothpick, you must bake for a few more minutes. Crumbs are ok, but not batter.

8. Cool for a few minutes. Loosen the edges of the cakes by running a knife all around. After cooling for a while, take them out from the pan and cool them on a wire rack.
9. Warm or at room temperature, these cheesecakes taste great either way. Place extra cakes in an airtight container. These can last in the refrigerator for about 3 to 4 days. Reheat and serve.

CHAPTER 2:
SNACK AND APPETIZER RECIPES

Turmeric Ginger Hot Cocoa

Serves: 1

Nutritional values per serving: 1 cup

Calories: 59

Fat: 4 g

Carbohydrates: 8.7 g

Protein: 2.4 g

Ingredients:

- ⅔ cup water
- 1 teaspoon grated fresh ginger
- ⅓ cup almond milk or oat milk or coconut milk
- Stevia drops to taste
- 1 teaspoon grated fresh turmeric or ½ teaspoon turmeric powder

- A pinch of freshly ground black pepper
- 1 teaspoon cacao powder or cocoa

Directions:

1. Boil water in a saucepan adding turmeric, pepper, and ginger. When it comes to a boil, take the pan off the heat. Let the flavors meld for 5 minutes.
2. Strain the mixture and add the liquid back into the saucepan.
3. Add cocoa, stevia, and milk and place it over medium-low heat. Stir often. When the mixture is warm, turn off the heat.
4. Pour into a cup and serve.

Hemp Hearts and Coconut Bar

Serves: 30

Nutritional values per serving: 1 bar

Calories: 218

Fat: 16 g

Carbohydrates: 10 g

Protein: 8 g

Ingredients:

- 2 cups unsweetened, shredded coconut
- 2 cups hemp hearts
- 2 teaspoons ground cinnamon
- 2 cups smooth almond butter
- ⅔ cup maple syrup

Directions:

1. Start by preheating the oven to 325°F.
2. Scatter the coconut flakes all over a baking sheet and bake until brown, about 5 to 7 minutes.
3. Combine hemp hearts, cinnamon, almond butter, and maple syrup in a bowl. Stir in the toasted coconut.
4. Place a sheet of wax paper in a baking pan. Spoon the mixture into the baking pan. Spread it evenly. Use the back of a glass and press the mixture. Chill until firm.
5. Cut into 30 equal pieces and serve. Store extra bars in an airtight container. They can last about 4 days at room temperature or 15 days in the refrigerator.

Apple Rounds with Peanut Butter and Pistachios

Serves: 4

Nutritional values per serving: 4 slices

Calories: 261

Fat: 13 g

Carbohydrates: 27 g

Protein: 10 g

Ingredients:

- 4 ounces of peanut butter
- 2 Gala apples or any other red apple of choice, cored, cut each into 8 slices crosswise
- ¼ teaspoon pepper
- ½ cup roasted nuts of your choice.

- 2 tablespoons honey

Directions:

1. Add peanut butter into a bowl and whisk until smooth.
2. Place the apple slices on a serving platter. Spread the peanut butter on each apple slice.
3. Top with pepper and nuts. Drizzle honey on top and serve.

Chocolate Chia Energy Bars

Serves: 7

Nutritional values per serving: 1 bar

Calories: 234

Fat: 12 g

Carbohydrates: 28 g

Protein: 4.5 g

Ingredients:

- ¾ cup packed, soft, pitted dates
- ¼ cup whole chia seeds
- ½ cup walnuts
- ¼ cup rolled oats
- ⅛ teaspoon sea salt (optional)
- 3 tablespoons cocoa powder

- ¼ cup unsweetened shredded coconut
- ¼ cup chopped dark chocolate
- ½ teaspoon vanilla extract (optional)

Directions:

1. If the dates you use are not soft, you need to soak them. Put the dates in a bowl of hot water and set it aside for 15 minutes. Drain off the water and use the dates.
2. Place walnuts in the food processor bowl and process until mainly coarse in texture, with a few small pieces.
3. Blend in the dates. Blend until the mixture is sticky. Add chia seeds, oats, salt, cocoa, coconut, chocolate, and vanilla, and blend until well combined. Take out some of the mixture and press it in your fist. If the mixture is sticking together, great, the mixture is perfect. If the mixture is crumbling on pressing, add a teaspoon or two of warm water and mix until the mixture has the right texture.
4. Place a sheet of parchment paper in a small baking pan with some of the paper overhanging from the sides.
5. Place the mixture in the baking pan and press it well. You can moisten your hand or use the back of a glass if required.
6. Freeze for about an hour or until it hardens.
7. Take it out of the pan with the help of the overhanging paper and place it on your cutting board. Cut into seven equal bars and serve.
8. You can place extra bars in an airtight container in the refrigerator or freezer.

Bell Pepper Sandwich

Serves: 2

Nutritional values per serving: 1 sandwich

Calories: 199

Fat: 20.1 g

Carbohydrates: 10.8 g

Protein: 20.6 g

Ingredients:

- 2 bell peppers, halved, discard seeds and stem
- ½ avocado, peeled, sliced
- 1 cup shredded spinach
- 1 tablespoon stone ground mustard
- 4 slices smoked turkey breast
- ½ cup sprouts

- 2 ounces of raw cheddar cheese
- ½ cup zero-carb mayonnaise

Directions:

1. Consider the bell pepper halves as your bread slices. Combine mustard and mayonnaise in a bowl.
2. Place 2 bell pepper halves on a serving plate, with the cut side facing up. Drizzle about a tablespoon of mayonnaise in each. Place half the spinach in the hollow of each bell pepper.
3. Place turkey, avocado, and cheese over the spinach. Place sprouts in a mound over the cheese. Drizzle the remaining mayonnaise on top. Cover with the remaining two bell pepper halves and serve.

Mushroom Quesadilla Bites

Serves: 8

Nutritional values per serving: 1 bite

Calories: 138.2

Fat: 5.3 g

Carbohydrates: 16.9 g

Protein: 6.4 g

Ingredients:

- 1 pound fresh mushrooms, sliced
- Salt to taste
- 10 tablespoons grated cheddar cheese
- 2 cloves garlic, minced
- 2 large whole-wheat tortillas
- Pepper to taste

Directions:

1. Warm the tortillas as per the instructions given on the package.
2. Place a non-stick pan over medium heat. Spray the pan with cooking spray.
3. Add the garlic and cook for about a minute. Add the mushrooms and stir on and off until there is no liquid left in the pan.
4. Add salt and pepper to taste.
5. Clean the pan and place it back over heat. Spray the pan lightly with oil.
6. Place a tortilla in the pan. Scatter half the cheese over the tortilla. Spread mushrooms all over the tortilla. Scatter the remaining cheese over the mushrooms.
7. Cover with the other tortilla. Press lightly to adhere. Cook until the underside is crisp and brown. Spray oil lightly on top of the quesadilla.
8. Carefully flip sides. When the underside is crisp and golden brown, remove it from the pan and place it on a plate.
9. Cut into eight equal wedges and serve.

Golden Glow Muffins

Serves: 6

Nutritional values per serving: 1 muffin

Calories: 181

Fat: 8.9 g

Carbohydrates: 21.9 g

Protein: 4.1 g

Ingredients:

- 3 tablespoons melted coconut oil
- ⅓ cup unsweetened applesauce
- ½ teaspoon vanilla extract
- 1 large egg
- 3 tablespoons pure maple syrup
- 1 cup plus 3 tablespoons oat flour or almond flour

- ¼ teaspoon baking powder
- ¼ teaspoon baking soda
- ⅛ teaspoon salt
- ¼ teaspoon ground cinnamon
- A pinch of freshly ground black pepper
- 1 teaspoon turmeric powder
- ¼ teaspoon ground ginger
- 3 tablespoons dairy-free chocolate chips plus extra to top

Directions:

1. Preheat the oven to 350°F.
2. Grease a muffin pan of 6 counts with cooking spray. Place disposable liners in each cup if desired.
3. Add egg, maple syrup, oil, applesauce, and vanilla into a bowl and whisk until smooth.
4. Combine flour, baking powder, soda, salt, ginger, turmeric, cinnamon, and pepper in another bowl. The pepper is necessary as it helps the body absorb the turmeric.
5. Combine the flour and egg mixture until well combined.
6. Distribute equally the batter among the muffin cups. Scatter chocolate chips on top.
7. Bake the muffins for about 20 minutes or until cooked through inside. To check if it is cooked through, insert a toothpick in the center of a muffin and take it out. If you find any batter stuck on the toothpick, you must bake for a few more minutes. Crumbs are ok, but not batter.
8. Cool for a fcw minutes. Loosen the edges of the muffins by running a knife all around the edges. Let the muffins cool for a while in the pan. Remove the muffins from the pan and cool on a wire rack for more time.

9. Place the muffins in an airtight container in the refrigerator until you need to use them. Serve warm or at room temperature.

Watermelon Walnut Salad

Serves: 4

Nutritional values per serving: ½ recipe

Calories: 215.5

Fat: 18.8 g

Carbohydrates: 8.4 g

Protein: 12.3 g

Ingredients:

- ⅛ watermelon, cubed, deseeded
- ⅛ cup chopped mint leaves
- 6 ounces mixed greens
- 3 tablespoons diced red onion
- 1 tablespoon lemon juice
- 1 tablespoon lime juice

- 1 ½ tablespoons extra-virgin olive oil
- 1 tablespoon apple cider vinegar
- A pinch of salt
- 3 ounces fresh mozzarella cheese or dairy-free cheese, diced
- ½ cup toasted walnuts chopped

Directions:

1. Combine mint, salt, and watermelon in a bowl. Let it rest for 30 minutes.
2. Drain the watermelon and add it to a bowl. Add mixed greens, onion, lemon, lime, oil, vinegar, salt, cheese, and walnuts. Toss well and serve.

Peanut Butter Fruit Sandwich

Serves: 4

Nutritional values per serving: 1 sandwich triangle without fruit

Calories: 194.4

Fat: 11.8 g

Carbohydrates: 16.9 g

Protein: 7.4 g

Ingredients:

- 4 slices whole-wheat bread
- Thinly sliced fruit of your choice like apple, strawberry, banana, or pear
- 16 teaspoons peanut butter

Directions:

1. Toast the bread, if desired, to the desired crispiness.
2. Spread 4 teaspoons of peanut butter on one side of each bread slice.
3. Place sliced fruit on 2 of the bread slices. Cover with the remaining 2 bread slices and complete the sandwich.
4. Cut each into 2 triangles and serve.

Raspberry Gummies

Serves: 8

Nutritional values per serving: ¼ cup

Calories: 45

Fat: 0.1 g

Carbohydrates: 11.1 g

Protein: 0.9 g

Ingredients:

- 1 cup kombucha or (a mixture of ½ cup kombucha and ½ cup pineapple juice)
- ½ cup raspberries or strawberries
- 4 tablespoons honey
- 4 tablespoons grass-fed gelatin powder

Directions:

1. Place the berries and kombucha in a blender and blend until smooth. You can use any other juice of your choice instead of pineapple juice. Pour the blended mixture into a small saucepan.
2. Cook the mixture over medium-low heat. Make sure it does not boil.
3. When it starts bubbling, whisking constantly, sprinkle gelatin over the mixture. If there are lumps of gelatin in the mixture, pour the mixture into the blender and blend until smooth.
4. Cook the mixture on low heat for about 40–50 seconds. Turn off the heat. Whisk in the honey.
5. Pour the mixture into molds and place in the refrigerator until it sets.
6. Remove the gummies from the molds. Cut into 1-inch cubes and store in an airtight container. They can last for about 15 days in the refrigerator.

Turmeric Chews

Serves: 55

Nutritional values per serving: 1 chew without honey

Calories: 13

Fat: 1.5 g

Carbohydrates: 0 g

Protein: 0 g

Ingredients:

- ¼ cup coconut butter
- 1 teaspoon turmeric powder
- A pinch of black pepper
- 2 tablespoons coconut oil
- ¼ teaspoon ground ginger
- 1 teaspoon honey (optional)

Directions:

1. Place the coconut butter in a heatproof bowl in the double boiler. The microwave is not to be used to melt the coconut butter.
2. Add coconut oil when the coconut butter nearly melts. Bring the bowl out of the double boiler, add the turmeric powder, pepper, ginger, and honey, and stir until smooth.
3. Pour the mixture into a baking pan. Cool in the refrigerator until it is firm.
4. Cut into 55 equal pieces. Separate the pieces and place them in an airtight container. They can last for two weeks in the refrigerator or two months in the freezer.

Avocado Hummus

Serves: 5

Nutritional values per serving: ⅕ recipe, without serving options

Calories: 156

Fat: 12 g

Carbohydrates: 10 g

Protein: 3 g

Ingredients:

- ½ can (from 15 ounces can) of unsalted chickpeas
- ½ cup cilantro leaves
- 2 tablespoons extra-virgin olive oil
- ½ clove garlic, peeled
- ¼ teaspoon salt
- ½ ripe avocado, pitted, peeled, chopped

- 2 tablespoons tahini
- 2 tablespoons lemon juice
- ½ teaspoon ground cumin

Directions:

1. Place chickpeas in a blender. Add a tablespoon of the canned liquid (from the can of chickpeas) into the blender. Also, add cilantro, oil, garlic, salt, avocado, tahini, lemon juice, and cumin and blend until pureed to smooth texture.
2. This can be served with vegetable sticks, pita chips, or crackers.

CHAPTER 3:
LUNCH RECIPES

Black Bean Quinoa Bowl

Serves: 2

Nutritional values per serving: 1 bowl

Calories: 500

Fat: 16 g

Carbohydrates: 74 g

Protein: 20 g

Ingredients:

- 1 ½ cups canned or cooked black beans, rinsed
- ½ cup hummus
- ½ medium avocado, peeled, diced
- ¼ cup chopped cilantro
- 1 ⅓ cups cooked quinoa
- 2 tablespoons lime juice

- 6 tablespoons Pico de Gallo

Directions:

1. Add beans and quinoa into a bowl and mix well. Divide the mixture into two serving bowls.
2. Add hummus and lime juice into a bowl and mix well. Add some water to dilute.
3. Spoon the hummus mixture over the beans mixture. Place avocado, cilantro, and Pico de Gallo on top in each bowl and serve.

Chicken Stuffed Peppers

Serves: 3

Nutritional values per serving: 1 stuffed bell pepper

Calories: 384

Fat: 19.7 g

Carbohydrates: 20.5 g

Protein: 32.9 g

Ingredients:

- 3 whole bell peppers or any color (you can use assorted)
- ¾ cup shredded mozzarella cheese
- 3 ounces pesto
- 1 chicken breast, cooked, shredded
- ½ cup cooked quinoa

Directions:

1. Set the oven to broil mode and preheat to high heat. Put the bell peppers in the oven and broil for 10 minutes until you see blisters and are slightly charred. Turn the bell peppers every 3–4 minutes so that it is cooked evenly on all sides. Turn off the broil mode.
2. Remove the bell peppers from the oven and set the oven to 350°F. Let it preheat.
3. Mix chicken, quinoa, pesto, and ½ cup cheese.
4. Let the bell peppers cool for some time. Cut each bell pepper into 2 halves. Discard the seeds and membranes.
5. Divide the filling among the bell peppers. Sprinkle the remaining cheese on top.
6. Place the bell peppers on a baking sheet, keep them in the oven, and bake for 8–10 minutes or until the cheese melts and is brown at a few spots.
7. Serve hot.

Tuna Salad Sandwich

Serves: 1

Nutritional values per serving: 1 sandwich without toppings

Calories: 420

Fat: 27 g

Carbohydrates: 2 g

Protein: 39 g

Ingredients:

- 1 can (5 ounces can) tuna in water
- 2 tablespoons mayonnaise
- Salt to taste
- Pepper to taste
- 2 whole-wheat bread slices
- 1 hard-boiled egg, peeled, diced

- 2 tablespoons chopped red onion
- Lettuce leaves
- Tomato slices
- Toppings of your choice

Directions:

1. Combine tuna, mayonnaise, egg, red onion, and seasonings in a bowl.
2. Toast the bread slices if desired. Place the tuna filling, tomato slices, and lettuce in between 2 bread slices and serve with toppings of your choice.

Chickpea Tuna Salad

Serves: 2

Nutritional values per serving: ½ recipe

Calories: 357

Fat: 19 g

Carbohydrates: 23 g

Protein: 21 g

Ingredients:

- 1 tablespoon lemon juice
- ½ tablespoon finely chopped shallot
- ½ can (from 15 ounces can) unsalted chickpeas, rinsed
- ½ cup halved cherry tomatoes
- ¼ cup crumbled feta cheese
- Pepper to taste

- 1 ½ tablespoons extra-virgin olive oil
- ½ tablespoon capers, rinsed, chopped
- Salt to taste
- ½ jar (from a 6.7 ounces jar) of oil-packed tuna, drained
- ½ cup thinly sliced English cucumber
- 1 tablespoon chopped fresh dill
- 1 ½ cups baby spinach

Directions:

1. To make the dressing: Combine lemon juice, shallot, seasonings, and capers in a bowl. Let it rest for 5 minutes. Add oil and whisk until well combined.
2. Mix well with tuna, chickpeas, cucumber, tomatoes, dill, and feta cheese in another bowl. Add 2 ½ tablespoons of the dressing to the tuna salad.
3. Pour the remaining dressing over the spinach and toss well.
4. Distribute the spinach equally and place it on two serving plates. Divide the tuna salad equally and place it over the spinach.
5. Serve.

Turmeric, Lentil, And Lemon Soup

Serves: 2

Nutritional values per serving: ½ recipe without yogurt

Calories: 172

Fat: 3.4 g

Carbohydrates: 26.2 g

Protein: 11.6 g

Ingredients:

- 1 teaspoon extra-virgin olive oil
- 1 ½ sticks of celery, finely chopped
- 1 teaspoon finely grated lemon zest
- ½ large onion, finely chopped
- 1 clove garlic, crushed
- ½ teaspoon turmeric powder

- ¼ teaspoon red chili flakes
- 6 tablespoons French green lentils, rinsed
- 2.3 ounces green beans, trimmed, sliced
- ½ tablespoon fresh lemon juice
- Plain yogurt to serve (optional)
- ¼ teaspoon ground cinnamon
- 1 cup vegetable stock
- 1 tomato, chopped
- 1.8 ounces kale, chopped
- 1 tablespoon chopped cilantro
- 1 ½ cups water
- Salt to taste
- Pepper to taste

Directions:

1. Add oil to a soup pot and place it over medium heat. Add celery and onion into the hot oil and stir until the vegetables are soft.
2. Stir in the lemon zest, garlic, turmeric powder, chili flakes, and cinnamon. Keep stirring for 30 to 40 seconds until you get a nice aroma, making sure not to burn the spices.
3. Stir in the stock, water, and lentils, and cook for about 15 minutes on low heat. Cover the pot partially while cooking. Add tomatoes and stir. Continue simmering until the lentils are cooked.
4. Stir in the kale and green beans. Cook for a few minutes until the beans are crisp and tender.
5. Add lemon juice and seasonings and stir. Add cilantro and stir.
6. Serve in soup bowls garnished with some yogurt if desired.

Pea Soup with Quinoa

Serves: 3

Nutritional values per serving: 1 cup without toppings

Calories: 126

Fat: 3 g

Carbohydrates: 19 g

Protein: 7 g

Ingredients:

- ½ cup water
- 1 teaspoon canola oil
- 1 ¼ cups frozen peas
- ¼ teaspoon salt
- ¼ cup dry quinoa rinsed
- ½ medium onion, chopped

- 1 ¾ cups chicken or vegetable broth
- ⅛ teaspoon pepper
- For toppings: Optional
- Nonfat yogurt
- Grated parmesan cheese
- Whole-wheat croutons
- Cracked black pepper

Directions:

1. Add water into a saucepan and place it over medium heat. Stir in the quinoa. Cover with a lid and cook until dry.
2. Place oil in a soup pot over medium-high heat. Sauté the onion in the oil and cook until pink, stirring on and off. Add broth and peas and wait for it to boil.
3. Turn down the heat to low and simmer until the peas are cooked. Blend the soup until smooth.
4. Add quinoa and seasonings and stir. Heat thoroughly. Serve in bowls with any of the suggested toppings if desired.

Spring Pearl Barley Salad with Ginger-Poached Salmon

Serves: 2

Nutritional values per serving: ½ recipe

Calories: 494

Fat: 19.6 g

Carbohydrates: 49 g

Protein: 33 g

Ingredients:

- ½ cup pearl barley
- 1.75 ounces green beans, trimmed, halved lengthwise
- ½ lemon, sliced
- 1.75 ounces broccoli, cut into small florets
- ¼ cup frozen peas

- 2 inches fresh ginger, peeled, grated plus ½ teaspoon extra for the dressing
- 2 skinless salmon fillets
- Few thinly sliced rings of small red onion
- 1 green onion, thinly sliced
- ½ tablespoon extra-virgin olive oil
- 1 tablespoon soy sauce
- Leaves of ¼ cos lettuce leaves, torn
- ½ tablespoon rice wine vinegar
- Water, as required

Directions:

1. Boil a pot of water with a teaspoon of water added to it. Add barley and cook until tender. Add the broccoli for 5 minutes and the peas for 2 minutes before draining off the water.
2. Rinse the barley mixture in cold water once the water is drained. Drain well in a colander.
3. Add 1 ½ cups of water to a pan while the barley is cooking. Add ginger and lemon and place it over medium-low heat. When the mixture starts simmering, turn down the heat and stir in the salmon. Cook the salmon until it flakes readily when pierced with a fork.
4. Fish out the salmon from the poaching liquid. Discard the poaching liquid.
5. Cut the salmon into bite-size pieces.
6. Add barley mixture, lettuce, salmon, and onion into a bowl and toss well.
7. Add ginger, vinegar, onion, and oil into a bowl and whisk well. Pour over the salad. Toss well and serve.

Black Bean Salad with Corn

Serves: 2

Nutritional values per serving: ½ recipe without toppings

Calories: 211

Fat: 12 g

Carbohydrates: 11 g

Protein: 2 g

Ingredients:

- ½ can (from a 15-ounce can) of black beans, drained, rinsed
- ½ cup halved cherry tomatoes
- 1 tablespoon diced red onion
- ½ cup fresh or frozen corn kernels
- ½ cup chopped bell pepper of any color
- ¼ cup chopped cilantro

For the cumin lime dressing:

- ¼ teaspoon ground cumin
- 1 tablespoon fresh lime juice
- Salt to taste
- ¼ teaspoon granulated garlic powder
- 1 tablespoon apple cider vinegar
- 3 tablespoons olive oil

Directions:

1. Add black beans, tomatoes, onion, corn, bell pepper, and cilantro into a bowl and toss well.
2. To make the dressing: Add lime juice, salt, garlic powder, vinegar, cumin, and oil into a bowl and whisk well.
3. Drizzle the dressing over the salad. Mix well. Let the salad rest for 5 minutes for the flavors to meld. Taste a bit of the salad. Add extra lime juice and salt if required, and serve with toppings of your choice.

Herb Avocado Sandwich

Serves: 1

Nutritional values per serving: 1 sandwich

Calories: 327.3

Fat: 17.24 g

Carbohydrates: 36.7 g

Protein: 10.2 g

Ingredients:

- ½ Hass avocado, pitted, sliced lengthwise
- ½ tablespoon chopped fresh cilantro
- A pinch of red pepper flakes
- ½ teaspoon unsalted sunflower seeds
- ½ tablespoon fresh lime juice
- ½ tablespoon chopped fresh basil leaves

- Salt to taste
- 2 slices whole-wheat bread

Directions:

1. Combine avocado and lime juice in a bowl. Add herbs, salt, and pepper flakes and mash with a fork until you get a smooth mixture.
2. Stir in the sunflower seeds. Smear the avocado mixture on a slice of bread. Cover with the other bread slice. Cut into the desired shape and serve.

Cucumber, Tomato and Arugula Salad with Hummus

Serves: 2

Nutritional values per serving: ½ recipe

Calories: 422

Fat: 30 g

Carbohydrates: 31 g

Protein: 11 g

Ingredients:

- 4 cups arugula
- ⅔ cup sliced cucumber
- ⅔ cup cherry tomatoes, halved
- ⅛ cup chopped red onion
- 4 teaspoons red wine vinegar
- ⅛ cup feta cheese

- ½ cup hummus
- 3 tablespoons extra-virgin olive oil
- ¼ teaspoon pepper
- 2 whole-wheat pita bread (4 inches each)

Directions:

1. Combine arugula, cucumber, onion, and tomatoes in a bowl. Drizzle oil and vinegar. Add pepper to taste. Toss well.
2. Divide the mixture into two plates. Scatter a tablespoon of feta on top of each plate. Place 1 pita bread on each plate along with ¼ cup hummus.

Pasta with Lemon Kale Chicken

Serves: 4

Nutritional values per serving: ¼ recipe

Calories: 692

Fat: 37 g

Carbohydrates: 59 g

Protein: 30 g

Ingredients:

- 8 ounces of whole-wheat pasta
- Freshly ground black pepper to taste
- 4 cloves garlic, minced
- 4 cups chopped curly kale, discard ribs
- 2 tablespoons lemon juice
- Salt to taste

- 2 boneless, skinless chicken breasts, sliced
- 10 tablespoons extra-virgin olive oil, divided
- ½ teaspoon red pepper flakes
- 1 teaspoon grated lemon zest
- Freshly grated parmesan cheese to garnish

Directions:

1. Place a pot of water with about a teaspoon of salt added to it over high heat. When the water starts boiling, drop the pasta into the pot and cook until al dente (according to the directions given on the package) but drain off a minute before the given time, retaining about ½ cup of the cooked water.
2. Heat a large cast-iron skillet over medium heat with 4 tablespoons of oil added to the skillet and wait for it to heat.
3. Sprinkle salt and pepper over the chicken slices and place in the skillet in a single layer. Cook until the underside is brown. Turn the chicken over and cook the other side until brown as well.
4. Take the chicken from the pan and place on a plate lined with paper towels.
5. Pour the remaining oil into the skillet. Add garlic and red pepper flakes to the hot oil and keep on stirring until you get a nice aroma, taking care not to burn it.
6. Stir in kale, lemon zest, salt, lemon juice, and retain pasta water. Once the kale is cooked, stir in the pasta and chicken.
7. Heat thoroughly, tossing on and off. Garnish with parmesan cheese and serve.

Cauliflower "Potato" Salad

Serves: 4

Nutritional values per serving: ¼ recipe

Calories: 183

Fat: 16 g

Carbohydrates: 6 g

Protein: 5 g

Ingredients:

- 4 cups cauliflower florets (bite-size pieces)
- ¼ cup thinly sliced scallions
- 1 ½ tablespoons dill pickle relish
- ¾ tablespoon coarse Dijon mustard
- 2 small hard-boiled eggs, peeled, chopped
- 1 tablespoon extra-virgin olive oil

- ¼ cup mayonnaise
- 1 tablespoon chopped fresh flat-leaf parsley
- ¼ teaspoon pepper

Directions:

1. Preheat the oven to 450°F.
2. Place cauliflower on a baking sheet. Drizzle oil over the cauliflower and mix well. Spread the cauliflower evenly without overlapping.
3. Place in the oven and roast for about 12 minutes or until the cauliflower is tender.
4. Take out the baking sheet and allow it to cool for about 15 minutes.
5. Mix well with cauliflower, scallions, and parsley in a bowl.
6. Mix well with mayonnaise, mustard, dill pickle relish, and pepper.
7. Add eggs and fold gently.
8. Serve.

CHAPTER 4:
DINNER RECIPES

Sweet Potato Black Bean Chili

Serves: 3

Nutritional values per serving: ⅓ recipe

Calories: 213

Fat: 0.6 g

Carbohydrates: 47 g

Protein: 6.8 g

Ingredients:

- ½ medium onion, diced
- ½ tablespoon coconut oil or olive oil
- 8 ounces salsa, preferably chunky salsa
- 1 cup vegetable stock
- 1 large sweet potato, scrubbed and cut into bite-size cubes
- ½ can (from a 15-ounce can) of black beans, drained

- 1 cup water
- Salt to taste
- ½ tablespoon chili powder
- ¼ teaspoon ground cinnamon
- Hot sauce to taste
- 1 teaspoon ground cumin
- ¼ teaspoon chipotle chili powder
- Chopped cilantro to garnish

To serve (Optional)

- Lime juice
- Avocado or guacamole
- Chopped red onion
- Any other toppings of your choice

Directions:

1. Add oil to a pot and place it over medium heat. Add onion to the hot oil, along with a bit of salt and pepper.
2. Stir on and off until the onion is pink. Stir in sweet potato, chili powder, cinnamon, cumin, and chipotle chili powder. Keep stirring for a few seconds until you get a nice aroma, making sure not to burn the spices.
3. Stir in stock, water, and salsa.
4. When the mixture starts boiling, bring down the heat to low and stir in the black beans.
5. Cook covered until the sweet potatoes are soft and can be pierced with a fork.
6. Turn off the heat and let it cool to room temperature. Let it rest for 5–6 hours in the refrigerator. This is done to make the chili more flavorful.
7. Heat the chili thoroughly. Serve with any of the suggested serving options.

Broccoli and Peanut Soba Noodles

Serves: 6

Nutritional values per serving: 1/6 recipe

Calories: 383

Fat: 14.1 g

Carbohydrates: 41.6 g

Protein: 18 g

Ingredients:

- 10.5 ounces soba noodles
- 2 cups broccoli florets
- 4 tablespoons smooth peanut butter
- 2 tablespoons rice vinegar
- 2 cloves garlic, crushed
- 6 spring onions, sliced

- ¼ cup roasted peanuts, chopped
- 2 teaspoons sesame oil
- 7 ounces edamame
- 2 tablespoons soy sauce
- 2 tablespoons grated ginger
- Lime juice to taste
- Lime wedges to serve
- A handful of chopped cilantro

Directions:

1. For the dressing: Add lime juice, ginger, soy sauce, vinegar, and garlic into a bowl and whisk well. Cover and set aside until you need to use it.
2. Boil a pot of water with about a teaspoon of salt added to it. Add the soba noodles into the pot and cook for about 4 minutes or until al dente. Add broccoli for 3 minutes and edamame for 30 seconds before draining off.
3. Drizzle sesame oil after rinsing (in cold water) and draining.
4. Transfer the noodles with vegetables into a large bowl. Add green onion and cilantro and mix well.
5. Pour dressing over the noodles. Mix well. Sprinkle it with cilantro on top. Serve topped with peanuts and lime wedges.

Mushroom Alfredo

Number of servings: 6

Nutritional value per serving: 1/6 recipe

Calories: 504

Fat: 14 g

Carbohydrates: 73 g

Protein: 21 g

Ingredients:

For the mushrooms:

- 2 teaspoons olive oil
- 14 cloves garlic, peeled, minced
- 2 tablespoons dry white wine
- ½ teaspoon dried thyme
- 1 medium onion, chopped

- 16 ounces mushrooms (white or Portobello or cremini or use a mixture)
- 2 tablespoons vegan Worcestershire sauce
- ½ teaspoon red pepper flakes or more to taste

For the Alfredo:

- 20 ounces fettuccine
- 2 small potatoes, cut into 1-inch cubes
- ½ teaspoon garlic powder
- ½ teaspoon onion powder
- 4 teaspoons lemon juice
- 1 teaspoon minced fresh basil
- 6 teaspoons extra-virgin olive oil
- Black pepper to taste
- 2 heaping cups of cauliflower florets
- ¼ cup hemp seeds or pumpkin seeds
- 1 ½ teaspoons salt
- 2 tablespoons nutritional yeast
- 2 cups water or cooked fettuccine water

Directions:

1. If you do not want to use hemp or pumpkin seeds, you can use cashews but soak the cashews in water for at least 30 minutes.
2. If you do not have vegan Worcestershire sauce, you can combine 4 teaspoons of soy sauce, 1 teaspoon of molasses, and 1 teaspoon of apple cider vinegar instead of Worcestershire sauce.
3. Boil a large pot of water. Cook fettuccine in boiling water for 3 minutes.
4. Drop the potatoes and cauliflower florets (do not make the florets very small) over the noodles.
5. Let it boil for about 6 minutes or until the fettuccine is cooked al dente or as you like.

6. Meanwhile, pour oil into a large skillet and let it heat over medium heat. When the oil is hot, add onion, mushrooms, and garlic and stir often until the vegetables turn golden brown.
7. Stir in Worcestershire sauce, wine, and red pepper flakes. Turn off the heat after about a minute.
8. Drain off the cooked water but retain about 2 cups of the cooked water. You need it to make the Alfredo sauce.
9. Pick up the cauliflower florets and potato cubes and place them in a blender.
10. Add the seasonings, lemon juice, extra-virgin olive oil, generous black pepper, hemp seeds, and nutritional yeast into the blender. Add about 4 tablespoons of the mushroom mixture and water or cooked pasta water and process until well pureed.
11. Add the blended mixture into the skillet with the remaining mushroom mixture.
12. Place the skillet over medium heat.
13. Let it simmer for a few minutes until heated thoroughly.
14. If the sauce is very thick, dilute it with water or vegan milk.
15. Add fettuccine and toss well.
16. Sprinkle basil and pepper on top and serve.

Butternut Squash Black Bean Enchilada Bake

Serves: 4

Nutritional values per serving: ¼ recipe

Calories: 378

Fat: 16 g

Carbohydrates: 43 g

Protein: 15 g

Ingredients:

For the sauce:

- 1 tablespoon olive oil
- ½ teaspoon smoked paprika
- ½ teaspoon sweet paprika
- ⅛ teaspoon red chili flakes
- Salt to taste

- ½ cup water
- ⅛ cup chopped cilantro
- 1 small onion, diced
- ½ teaspoon ground cumin
- ½ teaspoon dried oregano
- ⅛ teaspoon pepper
- ½ tablespoon jarred, minced garlic
- 1 ¼ cups tomato sauce

For the filling:

- 1 tablespoon olive oil
- ½ cup diced red bell pepper (½ inch dice)
- ½ cup finely diced onion
- ½ teaspoon sweet paprika
- ⅛ teaspoon red pepper flakes
- A pinch of salt
- ½ teaspoon ground cumin
- ½ teaspoon dried oregano
- ⅛ teaspoon pepper or to taste
- ½ can (from a 15-ounce can) black beans, drained, rinsed
- A handful of chopped cilantro
- 1 cup cooked, mashed butternut squash

To serve:

- 1 cup shredded cheddar cheese or vegan cheese
- 6 corn tortillas
- Chopped cilantro
- Salsa
- Chopped avocado
- Any other toppings of your choice

Directions:

1. To prepare the enchilada sauce: Add oil to a skillet. Place the skillet over medium heat. When the oil is hot, add on-

ion, cumin, pepper, red pepper flakes, oregano, smoked and sweet paprika, and stir for a few seconds until you get a nice aroma.

2. Stir in garlic. Keep stirring for a few seconds until you get a nice aroma, taking care not to burn the spices.

3. Stir in water and tomato sauce. Turn the heat to medium-low and cook for about 15 minutes or until the sauce is thick.

4. Add cilantro and stir. Turn off the heat.

5. To prepare the filling: Add oil to a skillet and place the skillet over medium heat.

6. Cook the onion in the hot oil for a couple of minutes. Stir in paprika, red pepper flakes, cumin, oregano, and pepper. Stir on and off for another minute or two.

7. Add about ¼ cup of water and dislodge any browned bits that may be stuck by scraping the bottom of the skillet.

8. Stir in beans and squash and heat thoroughly. Mash the entire mixture with a potato masher.

Quinoa with Chickpeas and Tomatoes

Serves: 3

Nutritional values per serving: ½ cup

Calories: 185

Fat: 5 g

Carbohydrates: 20 g

Protein: 31 g

Ingredients:

- ½ cup quinoa rinsed
- 1 ¼ cups plus ⅛ cup water
- ½ tomato, chopped
- 1 ½ tablespoons lime juice
- ¼ teaspoon ground cumin
- ¼ teaspoon chopped fresh parsley

- Salt to taste
- ½ cup cooked or canned chickpeas
- ½ clove garlic, minced
- 2 teaspoons olive oil
- Pepper to taste

Directions:

1. Add quinoa, water, and salt to taste into a saucepan. Place the saucepan over medium-high heat.
2. When the water starts boiling, turn down the heat to medium-low and cook until dry.
3. Turn off the heat. Mix well with chickpeas, garlic, oil, tomatoes, and lime juice. Garnish with parsley and serve.

Greek Chicken with Tomato, Olive, And Feta Topping

Serves: 2

Nutritional values per serving: ½ recipe

Calories: 405

Fat: 24 g

Carbohydrates: 5 g

Protein: 41 g

Ingredients:

- ¼ cup fresh lemon juice
- 1 teaspoon minced garlic
- 3 tablespoons sliced kalamata olives
- Salt to taste
- 2 boneless, skinless chicken breasts, trimmed of fat

- ¼ cup olive oil plus extra to cook the chicken
- 1 tablespoon chopped fresh oregano
- ½ cup chopped grape or cherry tomatoes
- ¼ cup crumbled feta cheese
- Freshly ground pepper to taste

Directions:

1. Score the chicken on top with a knife at a few places.
2. To make marinade: Add oil, oregano, lemon juice, and garlic into a bowl and whisk well. Retain 2 tablespoons of the marinade in a bowl and place in the refrigerator until you use it.
3. Place the chicken in a Ziploc bag. Pour the remaining oil mixture into the bag. Seal the bag and turn it around until the chicken is well coated with the marinade. Keep the bag in the refrigerator for 1–8 hours.
4. Let the chicken come to room temperature before cooking.
5. Add tomatoes, feta, olives, and retained marinade.
6. Add about ½ teaspoon of oil into a cast-iron pan and place it over high heat.
7. Take out the chicken from the bag and discard the marinade. Place the chicken in the pan with the scored side facing down.
8. Cook until the underside is brown. Turn the chicken over and cook the other side until brown and cooked through inside.
9. Transfer the chicken onto a serving platter. Sprinkle salt and a generous amount of pepper over the chicken.
10. Top with the tomato mixture and serve.

Chicken and Vegetable Soup

Serves: 3

Nutritional values per serving: ⅓ recipe without serving options

Calories: 300

Fat: 7 g

Carbohydrates: 29 g

Protein: 32 g

Ingredients:

- ½ cup corn kernels, fresh or frozen, thawed if frozen
- ½ tablespoon olive oil
- ½ cup chopped carrot
- 1 tablespoon tomato paste
- Salt to taste

- ½ can (from a 15-ounce can) of diced tomatoes with their juices
- 2 cups chicken stock
- ½ medium onion, chopped
- ¼ cup chopped celery
- ½ teaspoon granulated garlic powder
- 1 cup peeled, chopped russet potatoes
- 2 small bay leaves
- ¾ pound boneless, skinless chicken tenders
- 1 cup chopped green beans, fresh or frozen, thawed if frozen
- ½ cup peas, fresh or frozen, thawed if frozen

Directions:

1. Add oil to a soup pot and place it over medium heat. Add onion and salt when the oil is hot and stir on and off until slightly soft.
2. Stir in the celery, carrot, salt, and garlic powder and stir. Cook until the vegetables are slightly tender.
3. Stir in the tomato paste. Cook for about a minute. Stir in the potatoes, bay leaves, tomatoes, chicken, and salt to taste.
4. Pour stock and cook until it starts boiling. Now turn down the heat to low and continue cooking covered until the vegetables and chicken are cooked.
5. Fish out the chicken from the pot and place it on your cutting board.
6. Shred or chop the chicken into bite-size chunks. Add the chicken back into the pot. Also, add corn, beans, and peas and heat thoroughly.
7. Ladle into soup bowls and serve.

Chicken and Spinach Skillet Pasta with Lemon and Parmesan

Serves: 2

Nutritional values per serving: ½ recipe

Calories: 335

Fat: 12 g

Carbohydrates: 25 g

Protein: 29 g

Ingredients:

- 4 ounces whole-wheat penne pasta or gluten-free penne pasta
- ½ pound boneless, skinless chicken chopped into bite-size chunks
- Pepper to taste

- ¼ cup dry white wine
- 5 cups chopped fresh spinach
- 1 tablespoon extra-virgin olive oil
- Salt to taste
- 2 cloves garlic, minced
- Juice of ½ lemon
- Zest of ½ lemon, grated
- 2 tablespoons grated parmesan cheese divided

Directions:

1. Follow the directions given on the package and cook the pasta.
2. Place a skillet over medium-high heat. Add oil and let it heat. Place the chicken skillet. Add salt and pepper. Stir on and off for about 6 to 7 minutes or until the chicken is cooked.
3. Stir in the garlic. Keep on stirring for about a minute. Add lemon juice, wine, and lemon zest and stir.
4. When the mixture starts simmering, turn off the heat.
5. Add pasta and spinach and stir. Cover the skillet and let it rest for about 5 minutes.
6. Divide the chicken equally into two plates.
7. Sprinkle a tablespoon of parmesan on top of the chicken on each plate and serve.

Ground Turkey Sweet Potato Skillet

Serves: 2

Nutritional values per serving: ½ recipe, without optional ingredients

Calories: 294

Fat: 21.7 g

Carbohydrates: 41.4 g

Protein: 40.6 g

Ingredients:

- ½ pound sweet potatoes, scrubbed
- ½ teaspoon ground cumin
- ¼ teaspoon onion powder
- ¼ teaspoon garlic powder
- ½ tablespoon chili powder

- A pinch of cayenne pepper (optional)
- Fine sea salt to taste
- Freshly cracked pepper to taste
- ½ pound ground turkey
- ½ cup freshly grated sharp cheddar cheese
- 1 tablespoon olive oil
- ½ can (from a 15-ounce can) of black beans, drained, rinsed
- Chopped cilantro or parsley to garnish
- Fresh lime juice to serve

Optional ingredients:

- Cauliflower rice
- Chopped avocado
- Spicy mayonnaise
- For spicy mayonnaise: Optional
- ¼ cup mayonnaise
- ⅛ cup grated lime zest
- ⅛ teaspoon paprika
- ½ teaspoon hot sauce or sriracha sauce or more to taste
- 1 ½ tablespoons lime juice
- A pinch of ground cumin
- ¼ teaspoon chili powder
- A pinch of salt
- A pinch of pepper

Directions:

1. If you are making spicy mayonnaise, add mayonnaise, hot sauce, and all the seasonings into a bowl and mix well. Cover and set aside until the turkey skillet is ready.
2. Prick the sweet potatoes at several places with a fork and place them on a microwave-safe plate.
3. Cook in the microwave for about 8 to 10 minutes, turning the sweet potatoes every 3 minutes until they are tender and can be pierced with a fork.

4. Place a skillet with oil over medium heat. Add turkey to the hot oil and stir often until the turkey is nearly cooked. Make sure to break the meat into smaller pieces as you stir.
5. Discard any cooked liquids from the skillet if required.
6. Stir in the spices. Continue cooking until the turkey is now cooked well.
7. In the meantime, remove the peel from the sweet potatoes. Chop the sweet potatoes into cubes. Add sweet potatoes and beans into the skillet and stir the mixture well.
8. Heat thoroughly. Scatter cheese on top. Keep the skillet covered for a few minutes or until the cheese melts. Drizzle lime juice on top. Sprinkle cilantro on top.
9. Serve with suggested serving options if desired.

Turkey Teriyaki Rice Bowl

Serves 2

Nutritional values per serving: 1 bowl

Calories: 586

Fat: 28.1 g

Carbohydrates: 55.2 g

Protein: 31 g

Ingredients:

For coconut rice:

- ½ cup uncooked long-grain brown rice
- ½ can (from 13.6 ounces can) full-fat coconut milk
- ½ teaspoon kosher salt or to taste
- ⅛ cup water
- For the teriyaki sauce:

- 9 teaspoons soy sauce or tamari or coconut aminos
- 1 teaspoon sesame oil
- ½ teaspoon fresh ginger paste or ¼ teaspoon ground ginger
- 1 tablespoon honey
- ½ teaspoon garlic powder
- ½ tablespoon cornstarch or tapioca starch mixed with ½ tablespoon of water

For the turkey bowl:

- 1 small onion, diced
- ½ pound ground turkey
- ½ cup shredded carrots
- ½ tablespoon olive oil
- 2 cloves garlic, minced
- ½ cup chopped broccoli
- ½ red bell pepper, diced
- For the toppings:
- Diced avocado
- Sesame seeds
- Toasted panko (optional)
- Sliced green onions

Directions:

1. Add coconut milk, salt, and water into a pot and place it over high heat.
2. When it starts boiling, stir in the rice and lower the heat. Cook covered until there is no liquid remaining in the pot. Add some water if the rice is uncooked and there is no liquid in the pot.
3. Turn off the heat and loosen the grains with a fork. Cover and keep it aside for now.
4. In a bowl, make the teriyaki sauce by whisking together soy sauce, sesame oil, ginger paste, honey, garlic powder, and cornstarch.

5. To make the turkey skillet: Add oil and place it over medium heat.
6. Add onion to the hot oil and stir on and off until tender.
7. Stir in the turkey. Stir on and off until the meat is cooked, crumbling while stirring.
8. Stir in broccoli, bell pepper, and carrot. Cook for a few minutes until the turkey and veggies are cooked.
9. Add the teriyaki sauce mixture into the skillet and mix well.
10. Raise the heat to medium-high and cook until it is thoroughly heated.
11. Turn down the heat to medium-low and cook until the sauce is thick. Turn off the heat.
12. To assemble: Divide the coconut rice equally among two bowls. Divide the turkey equally and place it over the rice.
13. Top with avocado, sesame seeds, green onion, and panko if using, and serve.

Sheet Pan Shrimp Fajitas

Serves: 2

Nutritional values per serving: ½ recipe, without tortillas

Calories: 232

Fat: 7 g

Carbohydrates: 9 g

Protein: 36 g

Ingredients:

- ¾ pound shrimp, peeled, deveined
- ½ orange bell pepper, thinly sliced
- ½ red bell pepper, thinly sliced
- ½ yellow bell pepper, thinly sliced
- ½ small onion, thinly sliced
- 2 ¼ teaspoons extra-virgin olive oil

- Freshly ground pepper to taste
- ¼ teaspoon garlic powder
- ¼ teaspoon ground cumin
- ¼ teaspoon onion powder
- ¼ teaspoon smoked paprika
- 1 teaspoon chili powder
- ½ teaspoon kosher salt or to taste
- Lime juice to taste
- Tortillas to serve (optional)

Directions:

1. Set the oven to 450°F. Let it preheat.
2. Add onion, shrimp, and all the bell peppers into a bowl and toss well.
3. Drizzle oil over the mixture. Sprinkle all the seasonings and toss well.
4. Grease a baking sheet with some cooking spray. Scatter the shrimp mixture on the baking sheet and place it in the oven for 8 minutes.
5. Now set the oven to broil mode and cook for a couple of minutes or until the shrimp is well-cooked inside.
6. Drizzle lime juice over the fajita mixture. Sprinkle cilantro and mix well.
7. Serve over tortillas or lettuce leaves.

Fish Taco Bowl with Mango Salsa and Chipotle Aioli

Serves: 2

Nutritional values per serving: 1 bowl

Calories: 588

Fat: 46 g

Carbohydrates: 29 g

Protein: 24 g

Ingredients:

For the fish:

- 1 tilapia or cod or mahi mahi fillet (8 ounces)
- ¼ teaspoon smoked paprika
- ¼ teaspoon onion powder

- ½ teaspoon chili powder
- ¼ teaspoon garlic powder
- ⅛ teaspoon ground cumin
- ⅛ teaspoon pepper
- ¼ teaspoon salt
- ½ tablespoon coconut oil

For the aioli:

- 2 tablespoons mayonnaise
- ¼ teaspoon garlic powder
- ½ teaspoon chipotle chili powder
- 2 tablespoons full-fat coconut milk
- Salt to taste
- Lime juice to taste

For the guacamole:

- ⅛ cup diced red onion
- ½ tablespoon lime juice or more to taste
- 1 avocado, peeled, pitted, and chopped
- 1 tablespoon chopped cilantro
- Salt to taste

For the salsa:

- ½ tablespoon chopped cilantro
- 1 teaspoon lime juice or to taste
- Salt to taste
- ½ ripe mango, peeled, diced
- 1 tablespoon diced red onion
- For the cauliflower rice:
- 1 ½ cups cauliflower florets
- ½ tablespoon lime juice
- ½ cup full-fat coconut milk
- Salt to taste

For the cabbage slaw:

- 1 cup thinly sliced red cabbage
- Salt to taste
- ½ tablespoon lime juice

Directions:

1. To make guacamole: Combine onion, lime juice, avocado, cilantro, and salt in a bowl.
2. To make aioli: Blend mayonnaise, garlic powder, chipotle chili, coconut milk, salt, and lime juice until smooth.
3. To make salsa: Combine cilantro, lime juice, salt, mango, and onion in a bowl.
4. To make the slaw: Place cabbage in a bowl. Sprinkle salt and lime juice and mix well with your hands. As you mix, massage the leaves. Keep massaging for a few minutes until the cabbage is soft and the juices are released.
5. Mix well with salt and all the spices in a bowl to make the fish. Sprinkle spice mixture all over the fish and rub it well into the fish.
6. Place a skillet over medium heat. Add oil. When the oil melts, place the fish in the skillet. After cooking for about 3 to 4 minutes, flip the fish over and cook the other side for another 3 to 4 minutes or until the fish is cooked through. It should flake when you pierce it with a fork.
7. To make cauliflower rice: While the fish is cooking, place the cauliflower florets in the food processor bowl and process until the cauliflower is chopped to a rice-like texture. You can also use store-bought cauliflower rice.
8. Place a pan over medium-high heat. Add cauliflower rice, coconut milk, and salt, and often stir until the cauliflower is tender and nearly dry. Add lime juice and mix well.
9. To assemble: Divide the cauliflower rice equally and place it in two serving bowls in one half of the bowl. Divide equally and place the slaw in the other half of the bowl.

10. Place equal-sized portions of the fish in 2 serving bowls.. Place mango salsa and guacamole near the fish. Spoon the aioli on top and serve right away.

CHAPTER 5:
SIDE DISH RECIPES

Turmeric-Roasted Cauliflower

Serves: 2–3

Nutritional values per serving: 1 cup

Calories: 124

Fat: 9 g

Carbohydrates: 10 g

Protein: 4 g

Ingredients:

- 1 pound cauliflower, cut into bite-size florets
- 1 ½ tablespoons extra-virgin olive oil
- ¼ teaspoon ground cumin
- ¼ teaspoon pepper
- ¾ teaspoon turmeric powder
- ¼ teaspoon salt

- 1 large clove garlic, minced
- Lemon juice to taste

Directions:

1. Preheat your oven to 425°F.
2. Add oil and spices to a bowl. Mix well. Stir in the cauliflower.
3. Scatter the cauliflower florets on a baking sheet and place it in the oven.
4. Bake until they are brown on the outside and cooked through the inside.
5. Transfer the cauliflower to a bowl. Add lemon juice, toss well, and serve.

Catalan Spinach Sauté

Serves: 2 - 3

Nutritional values per serving: ¾ cup

Calories: 117

Fat: 6 g

Carbohydrates: 14 g

Protein: 5 g

Ingredients:

- 1 teaspoon extra-virgin olive oil
- 2 small cloves garlic, minced
- ⅛ cup currants
- Balsamic vinegar to taste
- ½ small onion, chopped
- ½ cup frozen, shredded spinach

- 1 tablespoon toasted pine nuts
- Salt to taste
- Freshly ground pepper to taste

Directions:

1. Add oil into a skillet and place it over high heat. Cook the onion in oil for a couple of minutes
2. Add garlic and stir. Cook for another couple of minutes.
3. Stir in spinach. Heat thoroughly. Mix well with currants, vinegar, pine nuts, and seasonings.
4. Serve hot.

Lemony Quinoa with Peas

Serves: 3

Nutritional values per serving: ⅓ recipe

Calories: 148

Fat: 5 g

Carbohydrates: 21 g

Protein: 6 g

Ingredients:

- ½ tablespoon extra-virgin olive oil
- 5 ounces frozen peas
- Zest of ½ lemon, grated
- ½ teaspoon salt or to taste
- ½ shallot, chopped
- 1 cup cooked quinoa

- ⅛ cup crumbled goat cheese
- ¼ teaspoon pepper or to taste

Directions:

1. Add oil into a skillet and place it over medium-high heat. Wait for the oil to heat.
2. Add shallot into the hot oil and stir on and off until it turns soft.
3. Add quinoa and peas and heat thoroughly.
4. Mix well with goat cheese, lemon zest, pepper, and salt.
5. Serve immediately.

Crispy Smashed Broccoli with Za'atar

Serves: 3

Nutritional values per serving: ⅓ recipe

Calories: 70

Fat: 5 g

Carbohydrates: 5 g

Protein: 3 g

Ingredients:

- 4 cups broccoli florets (bite-size florets)
- 1 teaspoon za'atar
- ¼ teaspoon kosher salt or to taste
- ⅛ cup low-fat plain Greek yogurt
- 1 tablespoon extra-virgin olive oil
- ¼ teaspoon garlic powder

- ⅛ teaspoon pepper or to taste

Directions:

1. Place 3 inches of water into a pot over high heat. Place a steamer basket in it and place the broccoli in the basket.
2. Steam for 3–4 minutes or until they turn just tender but not overcooked.
3. Meanwhile, place the rack 6 inches below the heating element in the oven. Set the oven to broil mode and preheat.
4. Combine steamed broccoli with oil and spread on a baking sheet. Take a mason jar and press each broccoli floret to smash.
5. Mix za'atar, salt, garlic powder, and pepper in a bowl. Sprinkle this mixture over the broccoli florets.
6. Place it in the oven and broil for 4–5 minutes or until they turn slightly brown.
7. Place a bit of yogurt on each floret and serve.

Marinated Tomatoes and Mushrooms

Serves 4

Nutritional values per serving: ¼ recipe

Calories: 106

Fat: 9 g

Carbohydrates: 5 g

Protein: 1 g

Ingredients:

- 2 tablespoons balsamic vinegar
- ¾ teaspoon brown sugar
- ¼ teaspoon pepper
- 3 tablespoons vegetable oil
- ¼ teaspoon salt
- 6 ounces cherry tomatoes, halved

- 1 green onion, sliced
- 4 ounces fresh mushrooms
- ¼ cup chopped fresh basil

Directions:

1. Add vinegar, sugar, pepper, oil, and salt into a bowl and whisk until sugar dissolves completely.
2. Stir in the tomatoes, green onion, mushrooms, and basil. Cover the bowl and place it in the refrigerator to marinate for at least 3 hours.
3. Give it a good stir and serve.

Sautéed Broccoli with Peanut Sauce

Serves: 3

Nutritional values per serving: ⅓ recipe

Calories: 154

Fat: 10 g

Carbohydrates: 12 g

Protein: 6 g

Ingredients:

- 4 cups broccoli florets (2-inch florets)
- ½ cup sliced red bell pepper
- 2 medium cloves garlic, chopped
- ¼ cup sliced onion
- 1 tablespoon toasted sesame oil
- 3 ½ teaspoons reduced-sodium tamari

- ½ tablespoon light brown sugar
- ½ tablespoon toasted sesame seeds
- 1 tablespoon rice vinegar
- ½ teaspoon cornstarch
- 4 ½ teaspoons smooth, natural peanut butter

Directions:

1. Place 3 inches of water into a pot over high heat. Place a steamer basket in it and place the broccoli in the basket.
2. Steam for 3–4 minutes or until they turn tender and crisp.
3. Add oil into a skillet and place it over medium-high heat. Add onion and garlic when the oil is hot and cook for about a minute.
4. Stir in the bell pepper. Stir often until the vegetables are slightly tender.
5. Stir in the broccoli. Stir-fry for about 2 to 3 minutes.
6. Meanwhile, add tamari, sugar, peanut butter, vinegar, and cornstarch into a small bowl and whisk until smooth. Pour into the pan with vegetables and mix well. Cook for about a minute or until the sauce is thick.
7. Garnish with sesame seeds and serve.

Tomato and Avocado Salad

Serves: 2

Nutritional values per serving: ½ recipe

Calories: 236

Fat: 22 g

Carbohydrates: 11 g

Protein: 2 g

Ingredients:

- ½ teaspoon Dijon mustard
- ¼ cup balsamic vinegar
- ½ avocado, peeled, sliced
- ⅛ cup extra-virgin olive oil
- A pinch of black pepper
- 1 medium tomato, cut into 8 wedges

Directions:

1. Add oil, mustard, pepper, and vinegar into a bowl and whisk well.
2. Combine avocado and tomato wedges in a bowl. Drizzle the dressing over the salad. Toss well and serve.

Roasted Savoy Cabbage with Orange Vinaigrette

Serves: 3

Nutritional values per serving: ⅓ recipe

Calories: 207

Fat: 18 g

Carbohydrates: 10 g

Protein: 3 g

Ingredients:

- 1 pound savoy cabbage
- 2 tablespoons orange juice
- ½ teaspoon minced shallot
- Salt to taste

- 3–4 drops of orange blossom water
- ¼ cup hazelnuts, toasted, crushed
- ½ tablespoon sumac
- 3 tablespoons extra-virgin olive oil, divided
- 2 small cloves garlic, minced
- ½ teaspoon white balsamic vinegar
- ⅛ teaspoon sugar
- Crushed red pepper to taste
- ½ tablespoon toasted sesame seeds

Directions:

1. Preheat your oven to 375 °F. Lay a sheet of foil on a baking sheet.
2. Lay the cabbage on the baking sheet so the stem side is down. Trickle a tablespoon of oil over the cabbage.
3. Place it in the oven and roast for about 1 ½ - 2 hours or until you can pierce a skewer easily through the cabbage.
4. Add 2 tablespoons of oil, garlic, vinegar, sugar, orange blossom water, orange juice, red pepper, and salt into a bowl and whisk well.
5. Add za'atar, sesame seeds, hazelnuts, and sumac into another bowl and stir well.
6. If there are any charred outer leaves of the cabbage, take them out and discard them.
7. Cut the cabbage into wedges. Sprinkle some salt over the cabbage. Trickle the dressing over the cabbage. Top with hazelnut mixture and serve.

Italian-Style Mushrooms and Spinach

Serves: 2

Nutritional values per serving: ½ recipe

Calories: 199

Fat: 14 g

Carbohydrates: 10 g

Protein: 6 g

Ingredients:

- 2 tablespoons olive oil
- 1 clove garlic, chopped
- 5 ounces fresh spinach, roughly chopped
- ¼ cup white wine
- Chopped fresh parsley to garnish
- ½ small onion, chopped

- 7 ounces fresh mushrooms, sliced
- 1 tablespoon balsamic vinegar
- Salt to taste
- Freshly ground pepper to taste

Directions:

1. Add oil into a skillet and place it over medium-high heat. Add garlic and onion into the skillet and stir. Cook until the onion is soft.
2. Stir in the mushrooms. Cook for a few minutes until some moisture is released from the mushrooms.
3. Add spinach and stir-fry until the spinach turns limp.
4. Stir in the vinegar. Keep on stirring until the mixture is dry.
5. Add white wine and stir. Turn down the heat to low and cook until nearly dry.
6. Add salt and pepper to taste. Garnish with parsley and serve.

Strawberry Tomato Summer Salad

Serves: 2

Nutritional values per serving: ½ recipe

Calories: 77

Fat: 3.9 g

Carbohydrates: 11.3 g

Protein: 1.2 g

Ingredients:

- 1 cup cherry tomatoes, halved
- ½ shallot, diced
- ½ tablespoon extra-virgin olive oil
- ¼ teaspoon pepper
- ½ pound strawberries, quartered
- 1 teaspoon lemon juice

- ½ teaspoon salt
- 1 tablespoon chopped fresh parsley

Directions:

1. Add tomatoes, shallot, strawberries, and parsley into a bowl and toss well.
2. Add oil, pepper, lemon juice, and salt and toss well.
3. Serve.

Mashed Sweet Potatoes with Ginger

Serves: 3

Nutritional values per serving: ⅓ recipe

Calories: 176

Fat: 4.6 g

Carbohydrates: 31.7 g

Protein: 2.6 g

Ingredients:

- 1 pound sweet potatoes or yam, unpeeled, cut into ½-inch thick round slices
- 1 tablespoon coconut oil or olive oil, or butter
- 1 teaspoon grated fresh ginger
- ½ teaspoon salt
- ½ shallot, finely chopped

- 1 clove garlic, minced
- Pepper to taste

Directions:

1. Place the sweet potatoes in a pot. Pour some water into the pot and cover the sweet potatoes. Place it over high heat. Cover with a lid.
2. When the water starts boiling, turn down the heat to low and simmer until the sweet potatoes are soft. Drain the sweet potatoes but retain some of the cooked water.
3. Place the same pot over medium heat. When the pot is dry, add oil. Add ginger, garlic, and shallots, and stir when the oil is hot. Cook until light golden brown. Stir on and off.
4. Add the sweet potatoes to the pot. Mash with a potato masher.
5. Add some of the retained water to get the desired consistency.
6. Add salt and pepper to taste.
7. Serve.

CHAPTER 6:
DESSERT RECIPES

Mini Blueberry Tarts

Serves: 9

Nutritional values per serving: 1 tart

Calories: 114

Fat: 5 g

Carbohydrates: 17 g

Protein: 1 g

Ingredients:

For the cookie crust:

- ¼ cup dairy-free butter
- ½ tablespoon unsweetened almond milk or soy milk
- ¼ teaspoon salt
- ¼ cup granulated sugar
- ¼ teaspoon vanilla extract

- ½ cup + ⅛ cup gluten-free flour blend

For the blueberry filling:

- 1 cup blueberries
- ½ teaspoon grated lemon zest
- ½ tablespoon cornstarch
- A tiny pinch of salt
- ⅛ cup granulated sugar
- ½ tablespoon lemon juice
- ⅛ teaspoon ground cinnamon

Directions:

1. To make the crust: Add butter and sugar into a bowl and beat until creamy and light with an electric hand mixer, about 2 to 3 minutes.
2. Beat in the vanilla extract, milk, and salt.
3. Add ½ cup of gluten-free flour and beat well until well combined.
4. Place the dough on a sheet of parchment paper. Flatten the dough until it is about an inch in height. Place it in the freezer for about 30 minutes.
5. In the meantime, prepare the blueberry filling: Combine fresh blueberries, lemon zest, cornstarch, salt, sugar, lemon juice, and cinnamon in a bowl.
6. Preheat the oven to 350 °F. Spray a mini muffin pan with cooking spray.
7. Take out the dough from the freezer and divide the dough among 9 cups of the muffin pan. It would be around a tablespoon per cup.
8. Now press the dough onto the bottom and a little of the sides of the muffin cup.
9. Place some of the blueberry fillings in each crust. You may have extra filling. That's ok but do not place the filling in a

heap. You can place the extra filling in a sealed container in the refrigerator. It can last for 3–4 days.

10. Place the muffin pan in the oven and set the timer for about 20 to 25 minutes until the edges of the crust are golden brown.

11. Cool completely and serve.

Avocado Brownies

Serves: 8

Nutritional values per serving: 1 piece

Calories: 130

Fat: 8 g

Carbohydrates: 13 g

Protein: 3 g

Ingredients:

- ½ large avocado, peeled, pitted
- 9 teaspoons coconut sugar or light brown sugar
- 1 ½ tablespoons dairy-free butter or coconut oil, or unsalted butter
- 5 tablespoons unsweetened cocoa powder
- ½ teaspoon espresso powder (optional)

- ¼ teaspoon kosher salt
- 1 large egg at room temperature
- 2 tablespoons pure maple syrup
- ½ teaspoon vanilla extract
- ¼ cup blanched almond flour
- ½ teaspoon baking soda
- ¼ cup dark or semi-sweet chocolate chips divided

Directions:

1. Preheat the oven to 350 °F. Place a sheet of parchment paper in a square baking pan (5 to 6 inches), so it is overhanging from 2 opposite sides.
2. Grease the parchment paper with a spray of cooking spray.
3. Add avocado, coconut sugar, butter, egg, maple syrup, and vanilla into a blender or food processor. Blend the mixture until you get a smooth puree.
4. Next, add almond flour, cocoa, baking soda, espresso powder, and salt and blend until you get a smooth batter.
5. Add half the chocolate chips and give short pulses until well combined.
6. Pour the batter into the baking dish. Scatter the remaining chocolate chips on top and place them in the oven for about 25 minutes or until cooked through. Insert a toothpick in the center of the brownie and take it out. If you find batter stuck on it, you need to bake for some more time (a few crumbs are ok but not batter).
7. Allow it to cool on your countertop for 25–30 minutes.
8. Pick up the brownies with the help of the overhanging parchment paper and place them on the rack. Cool completely. Invert onto a plate. Peel off the parchment paper.

9. Cut into 8 equal pieces and serve. You can place the brownies in a sealed container in the refrigerator. They can last for a week.

Pineapple Upside-Down Cake

Serves: 3

Nutritional values per serving: ⅓ recipe

Calories: 352

Fat: 23 g

Carbohydrates: 28 g

Protein: 10 g

Ingredients:

- ⅓ cup coconut flour
- 4 eggs
- A wee bit of salt
- ¼ can cored pineapple slices in juice
- ¼ cup coconut oil or softened butter
- 2 tablespoons honey or maple syrup

- ½ teaspoon baking powder
- ⅛ cup fresh cherries or maraschino cherries

Directions:

1. Preheat the oven to 325 °F. Grease a small, round baking dish or springform pan with cooking spray. Line it with parchment paper as well.
2. Place the pineapple slices on the bottom of the dish. Place a cherry in the hole of each pineapple slice (in the cored part). Place cherries in the gap between the pineapple slices as well.
3. Add coconut flour, eggs, salt, coconut oil, baking powder, and honey into a bowl and whisk until you get a smooth batter. If the batter is thick, add some pineapple juice (from the can) and stir until smooth. You need a batter of dropping consistency but not runny.
4. Pour batter all over the pineapple and cherries. Place it in the oven for baking for 25 to 30 minutes or until firm in the center.
5. Cool the cake in the baking dish itself for 8–10 minutes. Invert the cake onto a plate. Cut into 3 equal portions and serve.

Chocolate-Covered Banana Bites

Serves: 2

Nutritional values per serving: ½ recipe

Calories: 540

Fat: 29 g

Carbohydrates: 67 g

Protein: 4 g

Ingredients:

- ½ tablespoon coconut oil or vegetable shortening
- 1 banana, peeled, cut into 1-inch thick, round slices
- 6 ounces semi-sweet or milk chocolate chips

Directions:

1. Place a sheet of parchment paper on a small baking sheet.

2. Place banana slices on the baking sheet. Fix a toothpick into each banana slice and place it in the freezer for 30 minutes.
3. Meanwhile, add chocolate chips and coconut oil into a microwave-safe bowl and cook on High for about a minute or until the mixture melts completely. Make sure to stir the mixture every 15 seconds.
4. Take out the frozen banana slices. Pick one at a time, dip it in the melted mixture, and place it back on the baking sheet. Place it in the freezer if the chocolate doesn't harden for 10 minutes and serve.

Watermelon Sorbet

Serves: 4

Nutritional values per serving: ¼ recipe

Calories: 170

Fat: 1 g

Carbohydrates: 43 g

Protein: 3 g

Ingredients:

- ½ ripe watermelon, peeled, cubed, deseeded, frozen

Directions:

1. Process the frozen watermelon cubes in the food processor bowl until smooth.

2. Pour the mixture into a loaf pan. Place it in the freezer and freeze until you can scoop the sorbet.
3. Scoop and serve.

Apple Chips

Serves: 2–3

Nutritional values per serving: ½ cup

Calories: 65

Fat: 0 g

Carbohydrates: 18 g

Protein: 0 g

Ingredients:

- ½ teaspoon ground cinnamon or to taste
- 1 ½ large crisp apples like Fuji or Honeycrisp etc., cored, cut into ⅛ inch thick round slices crosswise with a mandolin slicer

Directions:

1. Preheat the oven to 200 °F. Lay a sheet of parchment paper on a baking pan.
2. Place the apple slices on the baking sheet. Dust with cinnamon and bake for about 1–1 ½ hours or until crisp, as you prefer.
3. Let them cool in the oven for one hour. Cool completely on your countertop and serve.
4. Place extra chips in an airtight container. They can last for about a week at room temperature.

Avocado and Strawberry Ice

Serves: 8

Nutritional values per serving: 1 container without maple syrup

Calories: 94

Fat: 7 g

Carbohydrates: 4 g

Protein: 3 g

Ingredients:

- 6 bounces strawberries, hulled, chopped
- 4 teaspoons balsamic vinegar
- 4 teaspoons maple syrup (optional)
- 2 avocados, pitted, peeled, and chopped
- 1 teaspoon vanilla extract
- 8 strawberries to decorate

Directions:

1. Add all the ingredients except maple syrup into a blender and blend until smooth. Taste a bit of it and add maple syrup only if required.
2. Pour into 8 small freezer-safe containers. Place one straw-berry on top in each bowl. Cover each with plastic wrap and freeze.
3. Let it thaw for about 5–10 minutes before serving.

Golden Milk Healthy Popsicles

Serves: 4

Nutritional values per serving: 1 Popsicle

Calories: 115

Fat: 10 g

Carbohydrates: 7 g

Protein: 1 g

Ingredients:

- ½ can (from 13.5 ounces can) of full-fat coconut cream or dairy-free milk of your choice
- ¼ teaspoon turmeric powder
- ½ teaspoon grated ginger
- 1 ½ tablespoons maple syrup or raw honey
- ¼ teaspoon cardamom powder

- A pinch of cayenne pepper
- Freshly ground black pepper to taste

Directions:

1. Blend coconut cream, spices, and maple syrup in a blender until smooth.
2. Initially, the coconut cream may separate into small bits, but no worries, continue blending until it gets smooth.
3. Transfer into four Popsicle molds. Insert the Popsicle stick in each mold and freeze until you need to use it.

Coconut Water Fruit Popsicles

Serves: 4

Nutritional values per serving: 1 Popsicle

Calories: 40

Fat: 0 g

Carbohydrates: 9.5 g

Protein: 0 g

Ingredients:

- 1 kiwi, peeled, chopped
- ⅛ cantaloupe, peeled, deseeded, diced
- 1 cup coconut water
- 3 strawberries, hulled, sliced
- A small handful of blueberries
- ½ tablespoon pure maple syrup

Directions:

1. Combine coconut water and maple syrup and pour into 4 Popsicle molds.
2. Divide the molds equally among the kiwi, cantaloupe, strawberries, and blueberries. Insert Popsicle sticks in each mold and freeze until firm.
3. Take out the required number of Popsicles and run under water for a few seconds. Unmold and serve.

Peach Berry Frozen Dessert

Serves: 18

Nutritional values per serving: 1 piece

Calories: 89

Fat: 2 g

Carbohydrates: 12 g

Protein: 6 g

Ingredients:

- 2 packages (8 ounces each) of fat-free cream cheese, softened
- 1 container (8 ounces) frozen light whipped dessert topping, thawed
- 2 cups fresh or frozen blueberries or raspberries, unsweetened

- Fresh berries to garnish
- 4 containers of peach fat-free yogurt sweetened with artificial sweetener
- 2 cups peeled, chopped fresh peaches or frozen unsweetened peaches
- Mint leaves to garnish

Directions:

1. Beat cream cheese and yogurt in a bowl with the help of an electric hand mixer set on medium speed. Beat until creamy and light.
2. Add whipped topping and fold gently. Add peaches and the berries and fold gently.
3. Spoon the mixture into a freezer-safe square dish. Cover it with foil and place it in the freezer for about 8 hours.
4. Take it out of the freezer about 45 minutes before serving, and place it on your countertop to defrost slightly.
5. Cut into 18 equal pieces. Top with mint leaves and extra berries, and serve.

Pineapple Nice Cream

Serves: 3

Nutritional values per serving: ½ cup

Calories: 55

Fat: 0 g

Carbohydrates: 14 g

Protein: 1 g

Ingredients:

- 8 ounces frozen pineapple chunks
- ½ tablespoon lemon juice or lime juice
- ½ cup frozen mango chunks or ½ large mango, peeled, chopped

Directions:

1. Add pineapple, lemon juice, and mango chunks into the food processor bowl.
2. Process until smooth and of soft serve consistency. If you are using frozen mango, you may have to add 2 to 3 tablespoons of water while processing.
3. Serve right away for soft-serve ice cream. For firm, freeze to the desired texture and serve.

CONCLUSION

Anti-inflammatory diets such as DASH and the Mediterranean diet can help you reduce inflammation and improve symptoms of various other health problems, including obesity and rheumatoid arthritis. This makes it a great diet to choose and follow as it does not have extremely rigid rules and instructions that you must follow.

There is no one particular anti-inflammatory diet, but rather any diet that contains fresh veggies and fruits, healthy fats, and whole grains and asks followers to reduce the intake of processed foods and red meats can be considered as an anti-inflammatory diet. It is highly recommended for people who have chronic inflammation. Yet, it is always best to talk to your healthcare professional before beginning any new health or diet regime.

This recipe book has been designed so you will never be confused about what to make to follow your anti-inflammatory diet. The recipes have been divided into multiple categories according to the meals. They are a wide array of recipes and dishes that are tempting and mouth watering and loaded with anti-inflammatory properties. Each recipe has been carefully crafted and curated with a special focus on fresh and whole ingredients known for their anti-inflammatory properties.

Whether a novice cook or an expert 'home chef,' these recipes are suitable for everyone and can serve as a step-by-step guide or inspiration to create new recipes on your culinary journey.

The book contains an amazing and rich variety of recipes suitable for pallets, tastes, occasions, and dietary preferences. From amazing snacks to breakfasts and brunch to main courses, the book contains recipes that will surely blow your mind.

It is recommended to keep an open mind while following the anti-inflammatory diet and try as many new food items, ingredients, and flavors as possible. This way, you might get introduced to your new favorite food!

This book will help you see positive changes in your life- one step and one recipe at a time. Let this book guide your journey towards a nourishing and delicious diet and allow foods to heal you.

REFERENCES

Ball, J. (n.d.). *38 Anti-Inflammatory Dinners You Can Make in 30 Minutes*. EatingWell. https://www.eatingwell.com/gallery/7946056/anti-inflammatory-dinner-recipes-in-30-minutes/

Cleveland Clinic. (2021, July 28). *Inflammation: What Is It, Causes, Symptoms & Treatment*. Cleveland Clinic. https://my.clevelandclinic.org/health/symptoms/21660-inflammation

Filson, M. (2022, August 16). *24 Anti-Inflammatory Recipes You Can Feel Great About Eating*. Delish. https://www.delish.com/cooking/recipe-ideas/g40847697/anti-inflammatory-recipes/

Raye, T. (n.d.). *Anti-inflammatory recipes*. Olivemagazine. https://www.olivemagazine.com/recipes/collection/anti-inflammatory-recipes/

Wartenburg, L., & Sprintzler, F. (2018). *13 Most Anti-Inflammatory Foods You Can Eat*. Healthline. https://www.healthline.com/nutrition/13-anti-inflammatory-foods

Printed in Great Britain
by Amazon